Original title:
Tales of the Tidal Pool

Copyright © 2025 Creative Arts Management OÜ
All rights reserved.

Author: Eleanor Prescott
ISBN HARDBACK: 978-1-80587-350-1
ISBN PAPERBACK: 978-1-80587-820-9

The Singing Sea Urchin

A sea urchin sat on a rock,
With a wig made of seaweed, not a sock.
It wiggled and jiggled, sang a tune,
Making fish giggle beneath the moon.

Crabs danced in time, clapping their claws,
While shrimps joined in with playful paws.
A starfish said, "Hey, that's quite the show!"
As barnacles watched from the ebb and flow.

Tides of Time

In a bubble of foam, sat a wise old clam,
With tales of the tides and the ocean's jam.
He chuckled and grinned as the waves rolled in,
Saying, "I've seen more than a fish with a fin!"

The sand dollars sighed, 'Time moves so slow,'
While snails in their shells whispered 'Let's go!'
They raced with the currents, oh what a sight,
As the tides of time danced day into night.

The Barnacle's Ballad

A barnacle perched on a ship's old hull,
Singing a ballad that echoed and cull.
With a voice like a trumpet, he wobbled and swayed,
His friends, the mussels, joined in the parade.

"I'm stuck here for life, but I've got some flair,
My songs bring the dolphins from everywhere!"
Together they laughed, the sea rumbled loud,
Who knew barnacles could draw such a crowd?

Moonlit Reflections on Water

Under the moon, the water did glow,
With fish in tuxedos, putting on a show.
They twirled and they spun, such dazzling sights,
As the octopus DJ mixed up the nights.

"Let's dance!" shouted clams, in shells shining bright,
While seaweed swayed in the rhythm of light.
Crabs made a conga, so silly and spry,
Beneath the moon's gaze, oh my, oh my!

The Winking Octopus

In a coat of vivid hue,
The octo shakes a leg or two.
With a wink that steals the show,
He dances slow, oh what a pro!

His arms are long, he likes to tease,
Sneaking snacks from fish with ease.
When all are full, he does a spin,
With eight-armed giggles, he wins again!

Saltwater Epiphanies

Upon a rock, a crab does pout,
He thinks of life, then spins about.
'Why scuttle here, just for a bite?
When I'd rather dance with all my might!'

A starfish sighs, it feels the strain,
'What is the point of this salty pain?'
But then it grins, a bright idea,
'Time to stretch wide, let's bring some cheer!'

Flickers of the Flickerfish

A flickerfish swims with flair,
Flipping fins in salty air.
With every splash, it starts to gleam,
Giggling loud, it's quite the dream!

It twirls and whirls in merry bliss,
Always stealing the limelight's kiss.
With a flip flop, it charms the crowd,
Making waves, oh, how proud!

The Tempest's Heartbeat

The waves crash loud, a wild parade,
As fish take cover, their plans delayed.
But hold on tight, for humor's here,
The tempest's giggle, loud and clear!

A seagull squawks, a jesting fool,
Riding waves, he breaks the rule.
In chaos lies a perfect jest,
For life's a splash, just like the rest!

Moonlit Murmurs

Under the silver glow, small crabs dance,
Flipping over rocks, they take their chance.
A sea star giggles, 'Hey, watch me twirl!'
While a clam just sighs, 'Oh, give it a whirl.'

Bubbles rise up from the kelp's long hair,
As fish play tag, without a care.
A wink from the moon, a splash in the night,
Nudging a sea urchin, it rolls with delight.

Beneath the Surface: An Ocean's Story

A snail in a shell thinks he's quite grand,
While a shrimp declares, 'Look, I can stand!'
An octopus chuckles, with ink in its pen,
'I'll write a new tale, time and again!'

Jellyfish jiggling, with grace on parade,
Whispering secrets of games that they've played.
With swirls of the tide, they dance and they twine,
'Are we underwater, or just sipping brine?'

The Forgotten Crevices

In the dark little nooks, critters have fun,
A pair of old gobies play peek-a-boo run.
Seaweed is laughing, tickling a crab,
While a flatfish grumbles, 'Oh no, a blab!'

Anemones tease with their colorful flare,
As barnacles settle without a care.
A curious snail shakes off the sand's weight,
'Is dinner at home, or is that too late?'

Jewel-tones of the Intertidal

With colors that burst like a piñata in sun,
Starfish and sponges say, 'Join in the fun!'
A sea cucumber wiggles, all jiggly and spry,
While the sea urchins pop, 'Just give us a try!'

The tide pools are laughing, it's time for a snack,
As seagulls dive in for a taste with a clack.
A romp through the waves, under skies so bright,
Underneath all the giggles, the sea feels just right.

Odyssey of the Octopus

In a cove bright and blue,
An octopus danced with a shoe.
It slipped on a crab,
What a funny fab!

With eight arms it twirled round and round,
Scaring fish that made silly sounds.
Old turtle just stared,
While jellyfish cared,

Sipping on tea served by clowns,
Before chasing seahorses in gowns.
Each marine delight,
What a comical sight!

So if you hear laughter so bright,
It's an octopus having a night.
In the waves up so high,
It's the best kind of spy!

Whirling in the Whirlpools

In a whirlpool, a fish took a spin,
Said, "Oh my, shall I ever win?"
He twirled with great glee,
It was quite a spree!

A crab joined the dance, feeling spry,
While octopuses cheered with a sigh.
Together they swirled,
With bubbles unfurled,

And the seaweed lay watching the fun,
As the whirlpool turned everyone.
Oh the giggles and grins,
These underwater wins!

With laughter and joy drifting free,
They spun like the leaves of a tree.
'Round and 'round they danced
In the deep sea's entranced!

Bottled Treasures

Found a bottle washed up on the shore,
With a message of fish wanting more.
Gull read it aloud,
Gathered a crowd!

It said, "Hey, we're planning a feast,
For the loudest clam who just won't cease!"
There's music and cheer,
With shrimp bringing beer!

A crab played the drums, quite bizarre,
While a starfish strummed on a guitar.
All the sea critters laughed,
At this homey craft!

So if you find bottles, take heed,
There's laughs and treasures, indeed!
In the ocean's vast dome,
Great parties can roam!

Wandering Sea Serpents

Two serpents set sail on a quest,
Searching for snacks, they were blessed.
They climbed a tall wave,
With rumblings so brave!

At a pirate ship's bow, they peeked in,
To see what funny chaos began.
With a swig of some rum,
They burst out in fun!

They tangled with nets, created a mess,
Turning sailors into a jolly dress.
'Twas laughter galore,
As they snagged some more!

So if sea serpents come near,
Just join in the fun, have no fear!
For their tales of delight,
Bring joy day and night!

The Sea Urchin's Grit

In rocky homes where sea urchins dwell,
They dress in spines, bark like they're swell.
A stubborn fellow, he'll not be moved,
With a wink and a grin, he's never disproved.

Clinging tight to rocks, he makes his stand,
With algae for snacks, he feels quite grand.
A crusty little sage in the bubbling tide,
With shells for his throne, he beams with pride.

Beneath the Surface: A Saga

Beneath the waves, a clam takes a nap,
While the crab sneaks in for a quick little tap.
"Excuse me!" says clam, "That's not very nice!"
Crab shrugs, "I thought it was quite a good slice!"

A starfish grins, saying, "Join in the fun!"
"You've got to be quick, or you'll miss the run!"
With jellyfish waltzing, they launch a new dance,
While seaweed twirls, giving all a chance!

Whirlpools of Ocean Memory

In whirlpools of laughter, the fish start to spin,
"I swear I saw you!" says a mullet with fins.
"Last week I was famous, a splashy delight!"
But the dolphin just chuckles, "All fish blend in tight!"

Shiny shells gather, gossiping low,
"Did you hear of the crab's dance with the blow?"
With colorful tales drifting 'round like the tide,
They giggle and jostle, with nowhere to hide.

Echoing Footprints on Wet Sand

Casting shadows where waves lap the shore,
The kids run and giggle, always wanting more.
With buckets and shovels, they dig and they play,
While crabs roll their eyes in a crustacean way.

The seagulls rejoice, "Look at their mess!"
"Every moment's a treasure, though I must confess!"
With laughter like music, the beach comes alive,
Where joy finds its echo, and silly dreams thrive!

Murmurs in the Shell's Embrace

In a shell that sat wide,
A crab whispered secrets so sly,
"I've seen fish wearing hats,
And jellyfish waving bye-bye!"

Starfish giggled at the tide,
As they slipped, with such flair,
A clam tried to dance nearby,
But tripped on salty air!

An octopus joined the show,
With eight arms making waves,
He juggled shiny seashells,
While the crowd cheered and raved!

Bubbles popped like fireworks,
As laughter filled the sea,
In a world under the foam,
Where nonsense runs free!

Reflections in Tidepools

In a tidepool full of glee,
A snail snapped a selfie, you see,
With a wink and a slimy grin,
He captured each ripple and fin!

Beside him, a fish in a tie,
Complained of the seaweed's sly,
"It's tangled in my new suit,
I can't let the crabs see this loot!"

A sea urchin popped out to shout,
"Don't fret! It's what it's all about,
Fashion's made of prickles and fun,
Now let's dance before we're done!"

As the sun began to set,
The tidepool echoed with laughter yet,
Where creatures shared jokes and tales,
In this world where joy never pales!

Guardians of the Shifting Sands

On the shore where sand meets sea,
Crabs held a council—it's true, you see,
With a crown made of driftwood and clams,
They proclaimed, "We're the kings of the jams!"

Seagulls mocked from high above,
"Your throne's just a pile of greased love!
But listen well, we share a joke,
About the fish who tried to smoke!"

As waves crashed, and laughter grew,
The sand made a mold of a shoe,
"Let's put it on a funny horse,
And see if that steed stays the course!"

When dusk painted skies so wide,
The guardians pranced, side by side,
With shells and laughter under the moon,
Singing tunes to the ocean's tune!

The Anemone's Secret Song

A bright anemone waved hello,
With tentacles dancing to and fro,
"I've written a song just for you,
About a fish who lost his shoe!"

Clownfish snickered as they swayed,
"Did it swim or get caught in a braid?
Make sure it's not a fancy dance,
Or it'll miss its chance to prance!"

In the current, the seaweed sighed,
"Let's invite the whole reef, come inside!
We'll throw a party, no time to stall,
With bubbles and snacks, we'll have a ball!"

The moonlit glow set the scene,
As laughter echoed, swirling between,
For in the depths of laughter's throng,
The secret of the ocean was strong!

Colors of the Undersea Canvas

In the tide's embrace, a crab wears a hat,
While starfish dance, oh what of that?
Fish giggle in bubbles, shimmering bright,
Colors so wild, they twinkle at night.

The seaweed sways with a twist and a turn,
As clams throw a party; oh how they yearn!
A dolphin shows off, does a flip in the spray,
While shrimps sing a song, making fun of the day.

With jellyfish gliding, all wobbly and round,
They float like balloons, never touch the ground.
An octopus doodles, in ink on the sand,
Crafting silly pictures, oh isn't it grand?

So join in the fun, don your goggles and fins,
With laughter and splashes, let the joy begin.
In this underwater realm, where whims always play,
Every wave brings a chuckle, come join in the fray!

A Symphony of Saltwater Shadows

Bubbles burst like laughter, what a joyful sound,
As fish take the stage, in their watery crowd.
A squid, wearing shades, plays the violin,
While seahorses waltz, let the laughter begin.

The sea stars clap with their tiny, bright hands,
While pufferfish puff, making all sorts of plans.
A hermit crab's solo brings down the house,
With rhythms so funky, that make us all douse.

With bubbles that sparkle like diamonds at play,
A mermaid joins in, her voice bright as day.
The corals all sway, keeping time with the beat,
As laughter erupts from the living sea seat.

In this underwater concert, where silliness reigns,
Funny fish tunes wash away all our pains.
So dive in and dance with all of your heart,
In this symphony of giggles, you'll play your part!

Legends from the Starfish Realm

In the kingdom of shells, where laughter prevails,
Starfish tell stories of far-fetched tales.
With six silly limbs, they gesticulate wide,
While squids roll their eyes, just shaking with pride.

A seashell, enchanted, holds secrets in rhyme,
As crabs gather 'round, all in their prime.
"Did you hear of the clam who sang high and low?"
They giggle and snicker, oh, how the tales flow!

The sea cucumbers whisper, their voices so low,
As they spin yarns of legends, with a rhythmic glow.
A turtle joins in, with a voice oh so grand,
Recounting the gossip spread throughout the sand.

So come take a seat, in the sandy old nook,
Where laughter and stories lure you like a book.
In this world of wonders, where fun never ends,
Every starfish has tales that it shares with its friends!

Driftwood Dreams and Ocean Schemes

On the shore, driftwood blossoms with dreams,
Where gulls plot adventures, or so it seems.
A lone sea otter, with a mischievous glance,
Plans a big party, complete with a dance.

With shells as their plates, they feast on some kelp,
While crabs do the limbo, oh what a yelp!
"Join in the fun!" the otter does plea,
"Be as silly as me; let's all just be free!"

The waves sway in rhythm, encouraging cheer,
As fish shimmy and shake, without any fear.
The clams chant along, keeping time with their clack,
While sea turtles float by in their own little pact.

So come to the driftwood, where dreams dance and play,
In this realm of the ocean, let silliness sway.
With laughter a-plenty and schemes in the breeze,
Join the driftwood's dreams; it's the best if you please!

A Symphony of Sand and Salt

The crab took a step, then a hop,
With a tap dance so grand, he wouldn't stop.
A seagull cawed, trying to sing,
But the crab stole the show, it was quite the thing.

The barnacles cheered, their shells in a clatter,
As a tiny fish joked, 'What's the matter?'
The waves laughed too, in their rhythmic tune,
While a clam tried to rhyme with a bright silver spoon.

An octopus juggled with shells on display,
As the tide pulled in, making waves at play.
The seaweed swayed like a dancer so bold,
In the sun's warm embrace, all stories unfold.

In this salty concert, the fun never ends,
With laughter and joy, everyone bends.
So come, take a seat on the warm sandy floor,
And let the ocean's humor be the lore.

Currents of Memory

A fish swam by, with bubbles galore,
Said, 'I can't remember what I swam for!'
The starfish giggled, 'That's quite a plight,'
While a hermit crab nodded, lost in the night.

The eel looked up with a shocking surprise,
'Why is that laugh such a wonderful guise?'
'It's simple,' said the fish, 'I just keep on drifting,
Through waves of old memories, my mind's gift is shifting.'

A sea turtle scratched his head in dismay,
'Every day feels the same in the bay.'
With a wink and a wave, the joke went around,
'Life's a big puzzle, but skip the profound!'

So if like a seashell, your thoughts start to sway,
Just float with the current and laugh all day.
For each wave that crashes holds stories to tell,
In the dance of the sea, we all know it well.

The Starfish's Secret

A starfish sly, with five points so neat,
Declared to the shore, 'I've got quite the feat!'
With a wink and a stretch, he wiggled with glee,
'I can change my color! Come, watch and see!'

The clams rolled their eyes, 'Oh, what a show!'
While the sea snails chased, moving painfully slow.
But the starfish, he sparkled, in hues of the bright,
'This talent of mine is pure delight!'

A jellyfish floated, perplexed by the fuss,
'What's the point?' she asked, 'Can't you just discuss?'
But the starfish just laughed, with a twirl and a spin,
'Life's a colorful joke, just let the fun in!'

So under the waves, the secret still blooms,
Where bright colors dance amidst seaweed's plumes.
In the laughter of tides, we find joy in the game,
For even a star can bring giggles and fame.

Gathering of the Shore's Spirits

Upon the warm sand, the spirits convene,
With shells for the seats, they prepare for the scene.
A crab with a hat, 'I'm the mayor today!'
Announced with a snap, 'Let's hear what you say!'

The sand dollars grinned, 'We bring the best news!'
'What's cooking today? Or do you have blues?'
A wave crashed in, with a voice like a kite,
'Spirits of saltwater, what brings you delight?'

The seagulls squawked in a raucous display,
As the barnacles chimed in, 'Hooray for the play!'
But the highlight was old clam with tales of the past,
His stories of tides that would alter so fast.

So under the stars, the evening took flight,
With laughter and cheers, hearts soaring in light.
For in every grain of sand lies a tale,
Of spirits that gather where the sea does exhale.

Echoes of the Shoreline

Seagulls squawk with delight,
Diving low, what a silly sight.
A beach ball rolls, then a shriek,
A splash of water, oh how bleak!

Laughter echoes, the tide comes in,
Kids build castles, let the fun begin.
A wave crashes, sand flies high,
A crab retreats, waving goodbye!

Fish flip-flop, making quite a scene,
A dolphin grins, what a silly marine!
With every splash, the giggles grow,
Who knew the sea had this much flow?

But beware of the jelly, oh so sly,
It looks like a sack, just floating by.
A twist and a turn, a wild chase,
Falling over, it's a slapstick race!

Crabs and Clams: A Coastal Chronicle

Crabby critters scuttle fast,
Hiding from the kids' loud blast.
Clams dig deep, but what a tease,
Just a shell in the sand, oh please!

The tide rolls in, crabs take a stroll,
One tries to dance but loses control.
With tiny legs, what a sight,
A crab in a clam—oh, what a fright!

Seashells chatter, secrets to share,
Underwater gossip fills the air.
A starfish waves from its rocky perch,
While fish play tag with a frisky lurch.

And when the moon shines bright and wide,
The crabs all gather for a moonlit ride.
As they tiptoe back, it's quite a treat,
With comical steps, they can't be beat!

Shells and Shadows

Shells all lined up, what a show!
Playing hide and seek, though they won't go.
A hermit crab peeks from a shell,
'This is my home, but all's not well!'

The shadows dance as the sun dips low,
A sea star twirls like a pro in the flow.
With laughter lurking behind each wave,
What secrets do these shells save?

Sandcastles crumble, laughter rings clear,
As the tide comes in, oh dear, oh dear!
The shells just giggle, they know the game,
They're not bothered; it's all the same.

So come to the shore where shadows play,
With every laugh, chase worries away.
Join the crabs, the clams, and more,
In this aquatic dance, let spirits soar!

The Dance of the Driftwood

Driftwood waltzes on the shore,
With a twist and a turn, it asks for more.
Seashell partners ready to glide,
In a sandy ballroom, they take pride.

A seaweed band strikes up a tune,
As crabs clap along under the moon.
Each wave a gardener, tending the floor,
While tides twirl round, oh what a score!

The driftwood bows, takes a spin,
It gleams and sparkles, what a win!
In the underwater lights, they all prance,
Every creature joins in this joyful dance.

And as the night falls, laughter remains,
The rhythm of the ocean, flowing in chains.
With every splash, they keep the beat,
A funny spectacle, none can beat!

Currents of Lost Stories

In the rock crevices lurked a crab,
Wearing a hat that looked fab.
He danced with a fish, oh what a sight,
Their giggles echoed, a joyful delight.

A starfish who thought he was a star,
Tried to hit the waves from afar.
He tripped on a shell, what a big splash,
As a clam let out a loud, heartfelt gasp.

A turtle named Timmy loved to race,
But he couldn't find his special place.
He ended up in a seaweed mess,
While jellyfish stung him—what a stress!

They gathered 'round, a critter convention,
With laughter and tales, oh what a mention.
In the currents, their stories would swirl,
Under the moon, they'd dance and twirl.

A Tapestry of Marine Whispers

Bubbles floated up with a sassy grin,
A shrimp took a leap, said, 'Let's begin!'
With a snail who thought he could sing a song,
But his notes, oh boy, were terribly wrong.

An octopus painted with colors wild,
Called out to a fish, 'Hey, you're my child!'
But the fish just swam, not wanting a mom,
While the octopus sighed, feeling quite glum.

There's a secret cave, they say, quite bold,
Where treasures are found, or so it's told.
But the treasures are socks and old bits of net,
The creatures all laughed, what a funny set!

With seaweed confetti, they danced in the tide,
Sharing their giggles with joyous pride.
In the currents they spun, their laughter a tune,
A quirky parade beneath the bright moon.

Whispers Beneath the Waves

In a sandy nook where the seaweed grows,
A sea cucumber tried on some clothes.
With a shirt from a clam and a tie quite strange,
It posed like a model, what a funny change!

The fish had a party in swirling delight,
With disco balls made of shells, oh what a sight!
But a seagull swooped in, hoping for lunch,
And they scattered away in a hurried bunch.

A sea horse named Sally danced on a shell,
Claiming she danced better than any other swell.
But when she tripped, oh dear, what a flop!
The crowd roared with laughter, 'You'll never stop!'

Yet beneath all their laughter and playful charms,
Was a bond of friendship, keeping them warm.
In the depths of the waves, where the stories bloom,
They created their joy, spreading laughter like a plume.

Secrets of the Seafoam

At the edge of the tide, a clam told a joke,
While a crab laughed so hard, he nearly broke.
The wave thrashed about, trying to listen,
As the starfish winked, his face all a-glisten.

A whale overheard and made quite a fuss,
He thought he was funny, but 'twas a big bust.
With echoes that traveled, they teased him a lot,
He belly-flopped back, leaving bubbles—a lot!

The sea anemone swayed to the beat,
Inviting all creatures for a toe-tapping feat.
They twisted and twirled, with barnacles clapping,
In the foamy white surf—a scene quite a-flapping.

So here in the waves, where laughter resides,
With friendships like pearls, and joy as their guides,
They shared every secret, each giggle, each sigh,
In the dance of the ocean, where spirits fly high.

Reflections in a Tide Pool

The crabs dance in their tiny shoes,
With sideways moves and silliness to choose.
Seashells gossip, sharing their woes,
While starfish giggle, striking silly poses.

A fish bumps its head on a barnacle wall,
And sea urchins chuckle, 'That's not so tall!'
The anemones sway, a colorful crew,
"Join us!" they call, "We're waiting for you!"

A small fish dives in, then quickly retreats,
Scared of the shadowed, lurking sea beats.
But the kelp is laughing, tickling the floor,
'The ocean is waiting, come in and explore!'

With pearls of laughter and bubbles of cheer,
The tide pool's antics bring joy, never fear.
As waves sing their songs, the tide's on a roll,
In this tiny world, there's fun in the shoal.

The Language of the Barnacles

Barnacles chatter, with shells on their backs,
They greet little waves with simple wise cracks.
Each time they are splashed, they giggle and cling,
'We love the ocean, it's a barnacle thing!'

They have secret meetings, held under the tide,
"Let's plot to play tricks!" one chirps with pride.
The mussels just listen, with shells tightly closed,
While the barnacles joke, their laughter exposed.

A crab scuttles by, with a scowl on its face,
"Why don't you all come join the sand race?"
But barnacles laugh, "We're firmly attached,
To swim like you, we'd need to be latched!"

In the dance of the tide, they wave little claws,
Barnacles banter, they hold no big flaws.
With snickers and nudges from creatures galore,
They claim their sweet kingdom, forever and more.

In the Thicket of Seaweed

In the seaweed jungle, a fish lost its way,
It thought it was dinner but turned out to play.
With fronds all around, it swirled and it spun,
'This salad's too tangled, I'm just having fun!'

A sea snail nearby offered some sage advice,
"Navigate carefully, here it can get dice!"
But the fish just wanted to play hide and seek,
In the green, wavy world, it felt so unique.

A seahorse giggles, stuck in a fray,
With sea cucumbers joining the fray.
They twist and they turn, laughing under the sun,
"This thicket is wild!" as they frolic and run.

From the top of the kelp, a bird lets out a squawk,
"Why's that fish dancing? It's supposed to just walk!"
But the seaweed shimmies, shaking all around,
In this whimsical thicket, the laughter resounds.

Nature's Underwater Theater

In the depths of the sea, the curtain it rises,
With fish in tuxedos and laughter surprise.
The octopus juggles all kinds of treats,
While seahorses dance, tapping wiggly feet.

The clam takes the stage, its voice really loud,
Singing ballads to the curious crowd.
But barnacles shout, "Can we have a dance?"
And the whole sandy floor gives sand critters a chance.

A seaweed curtain sways with a breeze,
As crabs play the drums, bringing everyone to their knees.

The show goes on, with jellyfish glow,
In this underwater theater, the laughter will flow.

At the end of the night, they all take a bow,
With bubbles and cheers, the audience wowed.
The tide rolls on in, still humming with cheer,
"What a fantastic show, let's do this next year!"

The Coral's Lament

Oh, the coral weeps in colors bright,
Fish get tangled in its funny sight.
Anemones dance, waving their arms,
While crabs scuttle by, with charming charms.

"Who wears the crown?" asks a starfish bold,
"I do!" shouts a clownfish, "Just look at my gold!"
The snails slide by with their homes on backs,
While sea cucumbers plot their sneaky attacks.

Seahorses giggle, all dressed up to play,
As jellyfish float in a wobbly way.
"Why don't we do a conga line here?"
"Only if you promise not to tickle my rear!"

The coral sighs, "I can't take the heat,
With all of you here, I'm losing my seat!"
But the laughter rings out from the tides so clear,
In this ocean of joy, there's nothing to fear.

Tide's Embrace

The tide rolls in with a giddy sweep,
Shells scatter wide, not a chance for sleep.
Crabs show off their best dancing legs,
While seaweed whispers, "I'm sprouting new pegs!"

"Is that a fish or a floating gumshoe?"
"Let's not ask questions; I'm hungry too!"
With a splash and a giggle, the dolphins dive,
Making the ocean feel so alive.

Barnacles cling with a stubborn pride,
"Hey, who invited all these folks outside?"
The answer, you see, is a wave and a grin,
As the tide rolls back, it just invites them in.

Each bubble that bursts sends laughter around,
In this watery world, joy knows no bounds.
With each wave that crashes, we dance and we sway,
In the embrace of the tide, we play every day.

Harboring Dreams

In the harbor spots, the fish have a scheme,
To host a grand party, 'cause it's a sweet dream.
The lobsters bring snacks, they're spicy and hot,
While octopuses juggle; they show off a lot.

The seagulls all squawk, "We'll steal the show!"
But the oysters snicker, "They can't put on a glow!"
With pearls shining bright, they craft necklaces fine,
And clams clink their shells, "Let's all sit and dine!"

The starfish encourage a game of charades,
While turtles play music with cool serenades.
"What a whacky gathering!" a crab exclaims,
"We should have a trophy for the funniest names!"

So they toast to the day with kelp in their cups,
And laughter erupts as the whole harbor hops.
In this dreamy harbor, the fun never ends,
With friends all around, it's the best that transcends.

Beneath the Salty Veil

Beneath the salty veil, life is a prank,
Fishes in hats hold a grand jamboree plank.
The eels tell tales with a giggle and twist,
While sponges soak up all the laughs that they missed.

"Let's go for a swim!" shouts a squid with glee,
As a turtle floats by, just trying to flee.
The flatfish camouflage, hiding their face,
While seahorses spin and glide with sweet grace.

"Who found the treasure?" a little shrimp squeaks,
"I think it was Dave, or maybe it's Cheeks!"
With bubbles and splashes, the fun starts to peak,
In this underwater world, they play hide-and-seek.

So under the waves, where the silly things dwell,
Life's a carefree dance, casting a spell.
With friends by your side, every moment feels right,
Beneath the salty veil, it's pure delight.

Echoes of the Forgotten Tide

Crabs in a race, who's the fastest?
Seaweed wigs on the playfully graspest.
Starfish cheers from a soggy perch,
While snails take bets in a slow-motion search.

Fish with hula hoops wave and twirl,
While sea cucumbers laugh at their whirl.
A merry dance where the bubbles burst,
Each creature's joy simply can't be curst.

Oysters wearing glasses sit very wise,
Dishing out pearls as their big surprise.
They giggle and wink, what a silly sight,
As seahorses prance in the moonlit night.

In this wet world, laughter is free,
Join the splash, come and see!
The humor drips like a soft ocean breeze,
In the ebb and flow, fear not the tease.

A Mosaic of Marine Myths

Mermaids host parties, oh what a craze!
With walruses dancing through misty haze.
A jellyfish serves a surprising snack,
While dolphins play tricks with a crafty knack.

The octopus juggles shells and dreams,
Spitting out water in shimmering streams.
Everyone giggles at tales gone wrong,
As seagulls join in with their squawking song.

Sea turtles gossip in shells they wear,
While shrimp shoot selfies without a care.
Each wave tells stories wrapped in foam,
Of hearty laughs from this bright underwater home.

And as the sun dips low in the sky,
The night sea creatures give a sly sigh.
With mischief brewing as the stars appear,
The ocean's mosaic dances with cheer.

Ocean's Heartbeat

Gulls have a chat about yesterday's catch,
While barnacles dream of a big, fancy patch.
Anemones giggle at every odd sight,
Waving their arms in a whimsical flight.

Clownfish laugh at their namesake tale,
Silly antics that never grow stale.
The waves crash down in rhythmic delight,
As the sea urchins chuckle all night.

Worms in the sand share secrets so funny,
While rays glide by, shining like honey.
A blenny will wink while adjusting his hair,
In this heartbeat of oceans, all humor laid bare.

With driftwood props and starry designs,
Creatures perform with their quirky signs.
In this vibrant show, laughter takes flight,
As the ocean's heartbeat echoes the night.

Guardians of the Shore

Crabs on patrol with tiny police hats,
Surveying their turf, while avoiding the flats.
Gull guides the flock, squawking his orders,
As clams gawk with their half-drawn borders.

Tide pools are trends, what's the latest style?
Starfish in sunglasses, they strut with a smile.
Sea anemones blush when the sea urchins tease,
As everyone's buzzing in salty sea breeze.

Sand dollars giggle, their tales seldom told,
While jellies float by, their laughter so bold.
Together they dance, though they're rooted in place,
As guardians of fun, in a sunken embrace.

So come take a look at these rascally mates,
Life in the tide is one that awakes.
Their antics bring joy, a splash to each shore,
In this world of whimsy, who could want more?

The Crustacean's Midnight Tale

Under the moon, a crab with flair,
Told jokes to the fish in the salty air.
"Why did the shrimp cross the road?" he grinned,
"To see if the tide made his shell feel pinned!"

A clam joined in with a wink and a laugh,
"I've heard better from a loaf of bread!"
The octopus snickered, his arms all a-dance,
"You'll need more than that for a proper romance!"

Thus laughter echoed, a bubbly delight,
As creatures played games in the shimmering night.
With shells all a-glimmer, they danced with glee,
A crustacean circus in waves of the sea!

And as dawn approached, the jokes came to rest,
The crab took a bow, and he felt quite blessed.
With one final jest, he waved them goodbye,
Till the next tidal wave would bring joy nigh!

Journey through the Seagrass Maze

Wander the seagrass, it's quite the spree,
Where fish play hide and seek with glee.
A starfish yawned, "Where's my coffee fix?"
"Just swim straight ahead, we'll find all the tricks!"

A jellyfish floated, all bouncy and bright,
"I swear these currents keep stealing my light!"
While turtles giggled, lost in their roam,
"We'll find our way back, just follow the foam!"

A sea cucumber said, with a squishy sigh,
"I'm too tired to move, let the current fly!"
But the giggling fish swam circles around,
In this seagrass maze, antics abound!

Eventually, they stumbled, a picnic in tow,
With seaweed wraps and a sand dollar show.
They feasted and laughed at their silly escapade,
In seagrass and bubbles, all worries unmade!

Colorful Lives Under the Seafoam

Deep in the blue, colors twisted and twirled,
A parrotfish danced, as bright as a world.
"Look at my scales, am I not a sight?"
"You shine like a disco in the moonlight!"

Anemones giggled, their tentacles swayed,
"If you think you're flashy, just wait for the parade!"
A clownfish chuckled, flipped in with style,
"With seafoam flair, I'll swim a whole mile!"

The sea turtle grinned, slow but so wise,
"Beauty is fleeting, just look at the skies!"
And mismatched the sea cucumbers danced,
In a wobbly line, as if by chance!

But under the waves, they all found their home,
In laughter and joy, forever to roam.
With the foamy embrace and vibrant display,
A lively concert in a watery ballet!

Moonlit Secrets of the Shoreline

Under the stars, the beach critters creep,
Sharing their secrets, as others all sleep.
A sand crab whispered, "I found a lost sock!"
"I thought it was lunch! Let's take it for a walk!"

With sea otters chuckling, they snatched up the find,
"Let's host a parade, it's one of a kind!"
And so they all gathered, from sand to the sea,
An unusual party, oh joy, oh glee!

An excited seagull squawked from above,
"Is this a sock dance? Oh, how I love!"
While the barnacles joined, with a clumsy clap,
In this moonlit revel, the turtle took a nap.

But the night faded fast, new dawn full of cheer,
As the crab held the sock, now full of sea beer.
They waved to the moon and thanked it for fun,
The shoreline is magic, where laughter's begun!

Chronicles Beneath the Waves

In a nook where the seaweed grows,
A crab tries on socks, just for shows.
With a snap and a clatter, he calls for a dance,
While octopuses giggle, not giving him a chance.

An oyster sings loudly, with pearls in her hair,
While seahorses gossip about a fishy affair.
A starfish suggests a seafood buffet,
But the clams just roll over, it's not their kind of day.

A jellyfish floats by, all dressed up for a ball,
But nobody will dance—can't feel a thing at all!
The hermit crabs chuckle, they just can't refrain,
"Why not join us, just trade for some grain?"

So the sea creatures gather, beneath the bright foam,
With laughter and bubbles, they feel right at home.
From a distance, the shore-watchers chuckle and cheer,
As a crab finds his footing—he's now the top tier!

Life Beneath the Barnacled Rim

Amongst barnacles, we find our fun,
Anemones laugh as the sea turtles run.
The urchins are poking, with quills all around,
While the clownfish wonders, "Where's my lost crown?"

A sand dollar chuckles, "I'm rich, can't you see?"
"But your fortune's in sand—you're as poor as can be!"
Starfish exchange winks as they tickle the tide,
While a pufferfish puffs, filled with ego and pride.

The crabs throw a party when no shells are in sight,
And dance on the rocks, with all of their might.
The flatfish just sigh, "Why can't we just nap?"
But the others keep giggling; they have no time for a map.

When the tide comes rolling and the laughter subsides,
They settle back in with the moon as their guide.
In the realm of the splash, where absurdity thrives,
Life beneath the rocks, oh, how humor survives!

The Coral's Quiet Confession

Corals whisper softly, secrets in hues,
Of fish with bad haircuts and tales of their shoes.
A parrotfish snickers, "Have you seen this array?
I'm quite the fashionista on my bright coral day!"

The clownfish are posing, all striped and so bold,
"Look at our antics!" is the story they've told.
But the corals just giggle, their stories quite sly,
"Wait till you see how the sea cucumber can fly!"

With a flip and a flop, the fish twirl in glee,
While a seahorse debates, "Should I wear polka dots or be free?"
The seaweed's a backdrop for a whimsical spree,
Where every bright creature can just be a 'she' or a 'he.'

So they dance and they frolic, through currents and tide,
With nothing but laughter as the ocean's guide.
In the corals' sweet warmth, there's a contagious delight,
For comedic confessions and adventures ignite!

Voices of the Crashing Surf

The sea roars with laughter, an orchestra live,
As seagulls tell stories that make the waves dive.
A shell chuckles, "Listen to that splashy confound,
All those fishes forming a band without sound!"

With a flip of their fins, the dolphins proclaim,
"We're the stars of this show! Isn't it all just a game?"
But the crabs are too busy, plotting a prank,
To snatch up the seaweed and hide in the plank.

The waves laugh and tumble, a joke in their churn,
As the sea stars reply, "Oh, you'll never learn!"
A surf clam recalls, "Do you remember when—
A sea cucumber tried to dance, with just one fin?"

When the tide pulls away, leaving stories in foam,
The laughter drifts softly, all creatures feel home.
For in this wild cycle, where time loses breath,
The surf tells the punchlines, from life until death!

Whispers of the Tide

In a shell so snug, a crab did natter,
He shared his thoughts on the fishy matter.
With pincers raised and a silly grin,
He claimed the tide was his best friend.

A clam chimed in, with a voice so low,
"I heard the seaweed has quite the show!"
They laughed so hard, they tossed and rolled,
With salty tales that never grow old.

The starfish giggled, stretched to the sky,
"Who knew the sea could tell such lies?"
Each wave brought chuckles, wild and free,
In this watery world, humor's the key.

So if you listen, on shores that gleam,
You'll find even fish enjoy a good dream.
Beneath the bright sun, with laughter rife,
The ocean's tales give sea critters life.

Secrets Among the Seaweed

In thick green strands, the gossip spun,
A flounder whispered, "I'm so much fun!"
The seaweed danced, swaying to the beat,
As fish exchanged jokes, oh what a treat!

A jellyfish laughed, it's true what they say,
"I'm the only one who floats all day!"
The octopus grinned with eight arms wide,
"You should see me at the tide's wild ride!"

Shells clattered softly, holding tales rare,
Of crabs that tripped on a twist of hair.
Every ripple carried giggles and grins,
In strands of seaweed, the laughter begins.

So if you wander close to the shore,
Join the whispers, you're welcome for sure!
Among the seaweed, fun's in the air,
Where secrets and laughter meet everywhere.

Echoes from the Rocky Shore

On the rocky ledge, with a bounce and a leap,
A seagull squawked, "I'm not one to sleep!"
He cracked a joke, all the waves did roar,
While crabs in their homes began to explore.

A fishy fellow swam by with flair,
"Did you hear that one? It's harder to share!"
The rocks held echoes of rib-tickling fun,
From surf's bright laughter, no one is done.

Anemones swayed, in a colorful crowd,
With the sea's comic spirit, they felt so proud.
The tides curled in, with glee and a twist,
Each splash was a chuckle, none could resist!

So gather 'round, with shells on your ear,
Listen closely, for the jokes we hold dear.
From rocks to the foam, let the laughter soar,
With echoes of joy from the shore to the core.

The Dance of Barnacles

In a cozy nook, barnacles pranced,
On the backs of whales, they gleefully danced.
With tiny feet tapping, what a sight to see,
These crusty little critters were wild and free!

As waves crashed down, they wobbled and spun,
"Hold on tight, this is lots of fun!"
The sea lettuce swayed, joining in too,
In this wacky waltz, all the ocean flew.

A seahorse joined, in his marvellous flair,
"Step to the left, if you dare!"
They twirled and they whirled, creating a spree,
With laughter and mischief, as light as can be.

So next time you wander, where water is warm,
Look for the barnacles, breaking the norm.
As they dance with delight on the ocean's grand floor,
You'll find humor thrives on the sea's playful shore.

The Secret Life of Sea Otters

In a cozy kelp bed, they lay all day,
Brushing fur, oh what a playful display.
With tiny paws, they crack open a treat,
Laughing as they slip, then dance on their feet.

With a pebble in hand, they're ready to dive,
Rolling and tumbling, feeling so alive.
Silly little acrobats, just having their fun,
Who knew being cute could be this much run?

They juggle their snacks, a show to behold,
Sea urchins and clams, treasures of gold.
Chasing each other through bubbles and foam,
In the soft sea spray, they've found their true home.

So next time you see them with seaweed in tow,
Remember these otters, putting on a show.
Their secret lives are a comedy spree,
In the watery world, they're wild and free.

Twilight Tides

As the sun dips low, the tide starts to play,
Crabs dance on the sand, come join in the fray.
With each little wave, they scramble about,
Bumping into each other, there's laughter, no doubt.

Starfish hang out, all stuck to the rocks,
Observing the antics of the silly flocks.
A seagull swoops down for a fishy delight,
But the fish laugh and dance, oh what a sight!

Glow of the moon, the sea sparkles bright,
Octopuses waltz in the soft, silver light.
Each splash is a giggle, each bubble a cheer,
In this whimsical world, there's nothing to fear.

So dance in the twilight with stars all aglow,
Join the merry creatures in their delightful show.
With a wink and a wiggle, let laughter ignite,
In the heart of the ocean, everything feels right.

The Shell Collector's Dream

With a bucket in hand, through the sand I will roam,
Searching for shells, my heart feels like home.
Each one a treasure, both quirky and round,
Laughing aloud, oh the joy I have found!

A razor clam giggles, it hides in the ground,
While the scallops all shimmer without making a sound.
I trip over seaweed, but oh what a sight,
I chuckle and tumble, and wear it with might.

A conch shell whispers, "Come play in the waves,"
While the busy little sand fleas are working like slaves.
I gather my finds, the funny and bright,
Each telling a story from day into night.

So let the waves crash, let the sea monsters play,
In my whimsical world, I find joy every day.
With each shell I collect, a new giggle in store,
In my shell collector's dream, there's laughter galore!

Chronicles of the Shimmering Shore

A hermit crab scuttles in a borrowed old shell,
Waving at beachgoers, giving them a yell.
"Hey there, come see my stylish new home!"
Scooting and sliding, he won't be alone.

Seagulls squawk loudly, stealing chips from the kids,
While the sunbathers chuckle, ignoring their bids.
With a flap and a flap, they dive and they swoop,
Crap! There goes my lunch, that cheeky bird troop!

Jellyfish float by, doing their jig,
While starfish applaud, feeling oh so big.
Crabs in their disco, with pincers in sync,
It's a party, my friends, come join in the wink!

So here on the shore, where laughter is free,
Every wave has a story, as funny as can be.
In the chronicles bright, life bubbles with cheer,
Join the fun on the shore: it's the best time of year!

The Lighthouse Keeper's Soliloquy

Upon my tower, I stand so proud,
Waving to ships, they cheer me loud.
Yet here I'm situated, all alone,
Just me and the seagulls who commandeer my phone.

The waves keep crashing with a funny sound,
A fish just leaped and spun around.
My only companion, a stubborn old cat,
Who insists on sitting right on my hat.

The beacon spins; it shines so bright,
While gulls play tag in the fading light.
I toss them crackers that fly like darts,
They squawk and squabble, true works of art!

At night I chat with the moon so wide,
As waves crash softly on the dark tide.
They say I'm mad, but I'm just a dream,
The lighthouse keeper of my own silly scheme.

Messages in a Bottle

I tossed my thoughts in a bottle one day,
Hoping the current would carry them away.
A fish took a nibble, then quick as a flash,
The message was gone—he must've made a splash!

I wrote to the mermaids, inviting them here,
But all I got back was a bubble and leer.
They must be quite busy, what with all the curls,
Or dodging the waves, those daring sea girls!

A crab found my bottle and claimed it as home,
Said he'd redecorate with seashells and foam.
I laughed at the sight, a true quirky guy,
Just living his life as the tide passes by.

So if you see bottles floating your way,
Just know it's my thoughts, in a funny display.
Some might get lost, but who really knows?
They could turn into stories, or ships made of prose!

Against the Coral Canvas

Coral shapes dance in the water's glow,
A painter's delight with colors in tow.
Starfish critique with their five-pointed views,
While eager shells giggle at all of their hues.

An octopus paints, quite abstract, I'd say,
With arms all a-splash in a colorful fray.
He grinned at the chaos, then turned to a shrimp,
"Now what do you think? A true artistic blimp!"

The clowns in the anemones chuckle with glee,
At the masterpieces churned up from the sea.
They tip over shells, creating a mess,
As if art's anticipated chaos meant success!

But amidst all the laughter, a close friend declared,
"Art's what you make it, so don't be scared!"
With each stroke of laughter, the coral shines bright,
In this underwater world of whimsical light.

Whims of the Wind and Wave

The wind blew funny, a mischievous chap,
Whisking my hat into an unplanned lap.
Seagulls just cackled, as waves rolled and crested,
In this ballet of nature, I felt quite vested.

The tide pulled back, revealing a joke,
A sunken old boot became a rude poke.
Shells chuckled softly, they whispered and shared,
"Who knew the ocean could be so unprepared?"

With every gust, a feathered friend zoomed,
Turning my picnic into seaweed's favorite room.
Sandcastles toppled in soft sandy waves,
And laughter erupted like the ocean's own braves.

Oh, whims of the wind and the playful surf,
Sketching up stories with giggles and mirth.
As the day drifts on, the sun dips and grins,
In this amusing kingdom where laughter still wins.

Crustacean Chronicles

A crab in a suit, so dapper and grand,
He struts on the sand, a ruler of land.
With sideways steps, he waves to the crowd,
While seagulls above squawk, 'Hey, look at him now!'

A lobster with dreams of becoming a chef,
Bakes algae pies, oh what a mess!
With bits of seaweed stuck on his head,
He serves them with flair but they're better off dead!

An octopus juggles, in water he spins,
His eight floppy limbs twirl, now here come the fins.
But flounders just frown, they shout, 'What a show!'
He slips on a shrimp, then—whoosh! Off he goes!

In the pool, there's a starfish with plans so surreal,
He tries on some shoes, now that's a big deal!
But he trips and he topples, so clumsy and round,
'That's one way to shine!' the sand dollars sound!

Surfside Serenades

A dolphin named Lou sings songs with a splash,
His notes float above with a bubbly gash.
While fish gather round, they dance in a loop,
'Til a whale rolls in yelling, 'Join in my scoop!'

The sand dollars giggle, all glitter and spins,
As clams start to bop, oh, what a din!
But a starfish takes charge, with rhythm so slick,
He twirls like a ballerina—oh, what a trick!

The waves join the dance, crashing with glee,
While barnacles cling like they own the sea.
A crab with a fiddle strums in delight,
But knocks over a mussel, 'Hey, that's not right!'

As the tide rolls in, the fun never stops,
With laughter and music, the water just hops.
Seagulls all chant, 'Let's do it again!'
And the sun sets on laughter where tides will reign!

The Quiet Conch

A conch on the shore, quiet and shy,
Hears all of the gossip that float and fly.
With thoughts of the ocean, and secrets to keep,
He listens to tales as the sea starts to sleep.

But one day a crab, quite raucous and loud,
Decided to dance and gather a crowd.
The conch set its sights, then heard something strange,
A clam in the back yelled, 'Let's make a change!'

Suddenly all shells began to unite,
With laughter and shouts that danced in the night.
The quiet conch chuckled, a smile on his shell,
Who knew silence could burst with such joy to compel!

As tides brought the moon and stars shone above,
They sang through the night, an ode full of love.
The quiet conch beamed with cheers from the band,
One tough little shell, now he's perfectly grand!

Twilight at the Waters Edge

As dusk settles in, the critters awake,
With shimmery scales and the spark of a flake.
A seagull tells jokes that make fish all snort,
While crabs roll their eyes, saying, 'What a sport!'

Old jellyfish bob, like lights in the dark,
They filter through secrets, so clever and stark.
With glimmers of laughter, they share silly puns,
As hermit crabs giggle, their shells full of fun!

A little flatfish hides, playing peek-a-boo,
While snails in their shells are giggling too.
The tide tosses in with a laugh and a swirl,
And shells start to twirl in a light, joyful whirl!

Oh, the night at the edge is a party, it's clear,
Where each wave whispers secrets for all to hear.
With friends in the surf, so silly and free,
They dance 'neath the stars, in their jiggly spree!

www.ingramcontent.com/pod-product-compliance
Lightning Source LLC
Chambersburg PA
CBHW060146230426
43661CB00003B/595